The Secret of Sales

"exposing the secret of sales in the business world"

Ben O. A.
Alfredo J. Chavez

Disclaimer Copyright

Contents

The secret of sales

- Talk to a career counselor
- Build your network
- Save money

Executing a strategy to love what you do

- To love what you do, strategize wisely
    a. Find a mentor
    b. Work with a coach
    c. Continue Innovative

- Develop positive habits
- Increase your passion for business by falling in love with your clients
- Give your credit for wanting to do what you love
- Appreciate your mistakes

Chapter 3

Building your career

- Highlight Your Goals
- Develop a Professional Resume
- Able to Identify your strengths
- Assume Full Responsibility for Your Life
- Always Raise Your Standards
- Brand Yourself
- Network — A LOT

Chapter 4

Networking

- What is Networking?

Types of networking

- Casual contact networks
- Strong contact networks
- Community service clubs

Chapter 5

Teamwork makes the dream work

- Why Teamwork Makes The Dream Work?
  - Motivation
  - Breaking Barriers
  - Enjoyment
  - Skill Improvement
  - Communication
  - Problem Solving
  - Bonding

Introduction

Even if you're new to the sales industry you know there's a core science behind it: prospect, lead, opportunity, pitch, close. However, you undoubtedly also know that it's not that straightforward. Sales aren't simply a science; it's also an art form. And like with any art form, some sales secrets may help you enhance your skill, and eventually, your statistics.

There are more ideas and methods than what we can cram into a single piece, but these 10 sales secrets will help your firm ascend to new heights almost instantly.

1. Create and manage an overflowing pipeline

While a large Rolodex alone doesn't lead to increased sales, it's a crucial beginning step. If you don't have expectations, you won't have buyers. In the beginning, it's easy to be distracted by earning money, but developing a pipeline is an investment in your career. You don't benefit from it immediately, but you'll earn significantly more in the long term than if you don't cultivate an audience.

2. Be more than a salesman

Salespeople strive to encourage prospects to purchase something. Business partners aim to demonstrate to prospects how they can profit from something. The first displays a transaction; the second, a connection. One of the most critical sales secrets is remembering that sales are about relationships first. Forget about the money. Worry about showing someone that you're there to make them succeed. Maybe they won't purchase now, but they could buy later or bring you to someone else who will.

3. Keep on learning

It's easy to feel that you've mastered the majority of what there is to know when you leave business school, but the fact is that the greatest salesmen never stop learning. Literature, webinars, conferences, and other educational materials will keep you ahead of the curve, which is likely to promote your company.

4. Be real, eager

These attributes appear less like sales secrets and more like common sense, but that's not always the case. Are you enthusiastic about what you sell? Are you driven, sociable, and outgoing? Is your excitement contagious? Do you exude charisma? Without authenticity, people are less inclined to trust you, and if they don't trust you, they aren't going to give you their money.

5. Raise your pricing

It is contradictory, yet studies have shown that many individuals regardless of costly items are of lesser quality than expensive ones. You want to stay within the market rate, but if you set your pricing a bit higher, people are more likely to recognize the value in what you're selling.

6. Focus on the negative

That's not to imply you should be negative. Focusing on the negative only means that you'll obtain more traction by illustrating how someone would be at a disadvantage if they don't purchase your goods. Showing people what they have to gain just piques curiosity, at best. Showing them what they have to lose will undoubtedly attract their attention.

7. Be generous

Have you ever heard of a client's product or service and known a great consumer for them? Inform your customer and offer to put them in contact. This and such similar altruistic activities show a customer you're not just interested in generating money, but in their success. Then, when they need your product or service, you'll be the first one they contact.

8. Make your shortcomings strengths

People are drawn to strength more than weakness. Turn any deficit into an advantage by showcasing the good where someone else perceives the negative. You can convert any weakness into a strength.

9. Ask, listen, reply

You'll lose fewer sales if you don't beg for the sale. You'll close even less if you accept no for an answer quickly. Ask for the sale, listen to arguments, and answer appropriately. Remember you want to assist your prospect to succeed more than you want to make a sale. Keep that in mind while you practice this.

10. Embrace failure

Even if you obey all of these sales tips, the fact is that you're not going to close every time. Don't sweat it. Take the failures as learning opportunities and don't be frightened to be turned down. Accepting rejection only makes you look more confident in a prospect's eyes, and if you're comfortable being turned down, it tells prospects that you believe in what you're selling.

Understanding the term Exchange

An exchange may be a physical place where traders convene to do business or an electronic platform. They also may be referred to as a share exchange or "bourse," depending on the geographical region.

An exchange is a marketplace where stocks, commodities, derivatives, and other financial products are exchanged. The basic role of an exchange is to provide fair and orderly trading and the efficient transmission of pricing information for any securities trading on that exchange. Exchanges provide firms, governments, and other organizations a platform from which to sell securities to the investing public.

An exchange is an open, structured marketplace for commodities, stocks, securities, derivatives, and other financial instruments. The phrases' exchange and market are sometimes used interchangeably since they both represent an environment in which listed items may be exchanged.

A primary role of an exchange is to offer fair, efficient, and orderly trading opportunities by centralizing the buying and selling of a certain kind of asset. Instead of dealing directly with exchanges, most traders will utilize a broker.

Secret tips to know:

1. Sell benefits, not features The largest error entrepreneurs make is in concentrating on what their product or service is. Rather, it's what it does that's significant, adds Tracy. That's what it is. What the product does is make the consumer leaner, more active, and able to achieve more with less sleep," he adds. "Also center on how your product will boost your consumer."

2. Sell to the ones most likely to purchase Your greatest prospects have a deep interest in your product or service and the financial means to acquire it. They are the ones who will purchase the fastest. "Sell to individuals who already have one, or to others you know might be interested in purchasing one. Show them how yours is greater."

3. Differentiate your product Why should a consumer purchase from you and not from your competitor? Tracy proposes coming up with at least three characteristics that will offer a buyer cause to purchase from you. "People don't want to move out of their consolation region to attempt something new. So, provide them three good reasons to try your product," Tracy says. "Your goods or help, for instance, performs quickly, is less expensive, and has a great quality degree".

4. Get face-to-face Spending big sums of money on print-media advertising or direct mail is one of the least effective techniques for first-time entrepreneurs to scale up their firms. There is no scarcity of emotional attitude. Get one-on-one with your customer—if not in person, at least through the phone.

5. Focus on the second sale Nearly 85 percent of all sales are gained via word of mouth. Therefore, concentrate on establishing future and

referral business with each customer. " Ask yourself: Will this be such a great experience that my customer will buy from me again or tell his friends?"

Examples of Exchange

Exchanges are present in most nations throughout the globe. They might be a physical venue, where traders congregate to do business or an electronic platform.

Physical
Electronic

Look forward as we launched our material.

Chapter 1

Success begins with the correct attitude

A good attitude provides favorable first impressions, which are the key to creating deeper personal and professional ties. Ultimately, this may generate in-roads in business, so that you can develop strong, enduring connections with employers, coworkers, and possible partners.

It's tough to be happy and fulfilled professionally (not to mention emotionally) if you're always overworked and stressed out. But there's a simple method to become both happier and more successful rapidly. It's as easy as this: adjust your mentality.

No, this doesn't imply you should stop attempting to develop or move ahead. Nor does it imply you should assume some kind of false, Ned Flanders-like persona. It simply implies that if you're able to alter your perspective to a place of appreciation and plenty vs scarcity and can adopt a positive attitude, your job may benefit in many ways.

Here are some of the ways that the correct mindset may make you more successful:

Create pleasant impressions.

You never have a second opportunity to create a first impression. It certainly comes as no surprise, but when you have a good attitude, you're more likely to portray yourself to people in a favorable manner.

Good impressions may lead to numerous possible rewards. Employers may be more inclined to pick you as a recruit. Co-workers, colleagues, and future partners will be more likely to collaborate with you.

On the other hand, if you have a negative mindset, you may experience precisely the opposite in all of these instances. When it's phrased like that, the option seems rather simple, doesn't it?

Deeper relationships.

A good attitude provides favorable first impressions, which are the key to creating deeper personal and professional ties. Ultimately, this may generate in-roads in business, so that you can develop strong, enduring connections with employers, coworkers, and possible partners.

Remember: when opportunity knocks, someone is doing the knocking. You want people to think of you when possibilities emerge, and your relationships are the key to making this happen.

You'll be more productive.
Everything is an uphill fight when you have a bad mindset. Picture the archetypal cranky employee who sighs every time he or she is asked to perform anything.

When you adjust your perspective, things will appear more doable and you'll be more optimistic about them. No, I'm not arguing that every activity will instantaneously become exciting rather than dull, or that you'll love every minute. However, you'll be more likely to perceive the advantages of getting duties out of the way so that you can get to the parts of your work you enjoy, so in that sense, you'll be more driven and productive.

Gain greater confidence.

If you want to be more confident at work, there are a range of activities that are shown to assist, from visualizing to enhance your posture to dressing for success. Unfortunately, none of these exercises will indeed be particularly helpful without the correct mentality.

When you have a positive attitude, you'll be more motivated to put in the effort required to practice self-improvement activities and to continue becoming stronger. In summary, an optimistic view will make it feasible to keep growing better, and this positive development will improve your confidence big time in the long run.

Stay devoted to your ambitions.

It can seem clichéd, but it's true: a can-do attitude can help you remain dedicated to your ambitions.

Setting precise objectives is an important practice for any business. However, when things go rough, it may be hard to stay motivated.
If you don't have the correct mindset, it might be simple to simply quit when things become rough. Because if you have a positive attitude, you're more likely to perceive your ambitions as worth continuing to strive toward. With this type of mindset, it's a lot simpler to keep going when challenges come.

You'll be happy.

By adopting the appropriate attitude, you stand to benefit in so many ways, but arguably the most significant is that it will make you feel better. When you feel better, things appear considerably more feasible in life. Day in and day out, they may have a dramatic influence on your job — and life.

So, consider shifting to an attitude of gratitude and applying it to your work moving forward. You have everything to gain!

The Benefits of a Positive Attitude for Entrepreneurs and Business Owners

Can having a positive attitude help your effectiveness in running your business?

The advantages of a good mindset in business
The advantages of an optimistic mindset include a feeling of optimism for the future. That sense of optimism leads to trust in the future success of commercial initiatives, regardless of the hard conditions of the present.

It's not breaking news, but most polls suggest folks prefer to work with someone positive rather than unpleasant. Interestingly, a more cheerful mindset may drastically enhance the judgments we make and the possibilities we seek. It also influences the individuals we interact with and the emphasis on our present objective. Finally, it favorably affects our drive to continue learning, and the development of our performance.

High performers

Research by psychologist Marcial Losada indicated various possible advantages businesses may enjoy with a more cheerful mindset. For instance, it makes you more interested, keener to explore, and eager to take the initiative. You're more open to new ideas, relationships with new people, and attempting new activities.

Additionally, the study showed that a negative attitude limits your experience and holds you back. It puts you in a “leave me alone” mode. Some refer to this mode as a “bunker mentality,” where you’re always on guard and defensive. The study further revealed that a more negative attitude changes your worldview and how you interact with others. It limits your possibilities and undermines your self-esteem.

Expanded awareness

I recently viewed a series of lectures delivered by Barbara Frederickson, Ph.D. Frederickson is the author of Positivity. She serves as the Kenan Distinguished Professor and Director of Positive Emotions and Psychophysiology at the University of North Carolina at Chapel Hill.

Frederickson’s research indicates that a positive attitude expands our awareness and “makes our world larger.” She also concluded that to stay on the positive side and maintain this expanded awareness, we need to adopt a positive attitude in three events to every negative event. Surprisingly, only one in five people surveyed met this 3-to-1 ratio.

Additional benefits

These include a capacity for more ideas, greater creativity, and improved resilience. Moreover, it embraces a higher readiness to build a win-win mentality amid stress and disagreement.

Some criticism keeps an entrepreneur grounded. However, you don't want to get so disheartened that you lock yourself into an unending spiral of negativity. A negative attitude may quickly overpower you, and this often occurs when you neglect to check if the thoughts underlying your bad attitude are genuine.

A cheerful attitude in a world that looks out of control

A cheerful mindset doesn't simply happen on its own. You need to leave the negativity behind, let it go, and proactively do good, useful things. These items might include completing tasks and projects, launching new enterprises, and handling customer-related concerns.

We're ultimately in charge of whether we choose to approach our daily tasks with a good attitude or yield to a more negative perspective.

Chapter 2

LOVE WHAT YOU DO

You've heard the adage, "Do what you love and you'll never work a day in your life." In many respects, this phrase is accurate. If you're enthusiastic about what you do and you're pouring your concentration and energy into it, you won't feel like you're working. Yet many individuals exploit this philosophy as an excuse. Why devote time and effort to something if you don't enjoy it?

The reality is, if you enjoy what you do for a job, you probably began by taking tiny efforts to accomplish that objective.
Most individuals don't begin their employment and instantly have a love for business.
What is the IT element these individuals have in common? Purpose. If you utilize your sense of purpose to influence your professional choices and advancement, you will wind up teaching yourself how to accomplish what you love.

To be true to your purpose as it pertains to your life's work, which is crucial to developing a profession in which you genuinely enjoy what you do, then you need to ask yourself, "What is my inner potential, and what are my core talents?" By studying questions that push you to identify your identity, values, and what you care about the most, you'll learn the reality that you must first comprehend what your true talent is to obtain fulfillment in your work.

As Tony Robbins says, "Change is automatic, but progress is not. If you want to achieve progress, you need a plan, a strategy, and continuous behaviors to obtain the outcomes you desire." We'll break down these components and examine how they're required if you want to do what you love and enjoy what you do.

Learning how to do what you love

If you're intimidated by the notion of making big adjustments to do what you love for a job, take tiny steps. Getting to know yourself is the first step in learning to enjoy what you do. Here are some strategies to come in touch with what motivates you.

1. Focus on your strength

Knowing what you love to do is a prerequisite for learning how to do it well. This is a process of self-discovery that brings you in touch with your essential values, strengths, and assets. In his Building the Ultimate Business Advantage course, marketing guru Jay Abraham claims that many entrepreneurs are dissatisfied because they are continuously attempting to fix their flaws.
Jay supports concentrating on your talents when determining what sort of company to start and having a development plan in place. When you determine what you like doing and the tasks

you're able to master reasonably fast, you'll experience more significant achievements that lead to satisfaction.

Creating a profession where you do what you love for a livelihood is about spending the bulk of your time practicing and acting on your talents. This isn't simply a formula for growing your love for business, though - when prospective consumers realize how enthusiastic you are, they're more likely to catch on, which drastically raises your likelihood of company success.

2. Find your passion

The next stage in building a job in which you enjoy what you do is in thinking carefully about your mission. What inspires you? What do you wish you could get up and do every day?
These replies must fall by what your strengths are. For some individuals, the opportunity to accomplish what they love involves assisting others. For a different individual, it's expressing their ideas and emotions artistically. Others value travel or spending time with their family. Once you've thought about what living an outstanding life looks like for you, explore how you'll attain it.

3. Talk to a career counselor

Working with a career counselor is a fantastic approach to fine-tune your professional path. Career counselors are educated to help clients in the greatest possible way toward self-actualization. An experienced career counselor assesses your talents, background, inspirations, and personality qualities to assist create a plan of action to accomplish what you love.

4. Build your network

When you're in the process of shifting your profession to do what you love, now is the time to create contacts and develop your network. When you reach out to others – particularly those you admire who've discovered solutions to how to accomplish what you love – you tap into a wellspring of support, knowledge, and inspiration. Then, when you go to apply your plan for professional satisfaction, your network will be ready and waiting.

5. Save money

As you seek to develop a profession that enables you to do what you love, be smart about your money so your resources are focused on the goal. Prioritize your expenditures on activities that support your hobbies. You'll boost your feeling of self-efficacy while maintaining resources to realize your ambitions.

Executing a strategy to love what you do

You've already put in the leg work required to pursue what you love. Your next stage is formulating a plan for getting there. This is your action plan for learning how to do what you love and enjoy what you do.

1. To love what you do, strategize wisely

Unless you're born into money, you're going to have to work to be able to accomplish what you love. Begin with a plan – or better yet, a Huge Action Plan.
How can you accomplish your actual purpose via work? How do you merge that passion with a real-world career? Plan how you can make your idea a reality.

You're never going to get from point A, as a total novice, to point Z, in which you suddenly get to do what you love and have achieved full financial independence. You have to plan carefully to travel from point A to point B to point C, and so on. How can you most effectively develop a profession in which you enjoy what you do?

There are a few actions you may take to speed up this process:

Find a method

Whether it's someone you know in real life who has achieved huge success or someone you haven't met in person but truly like, find out how they discovered success. Ask them what steps they took to find how to accomplish what they love, then ask yourself how you may mimic the route they followed with adaptations to match your circumstances. Almost every successful business person – including Tony – has been trained by mentors throughout their lives.

Walk with a coach

If you don't have the skills to do what you love and establish a company around it on your own, don't worry: There is plenty of support available. Work with a Results Coach who can help you concentrate on your ultimate goal and support you in establishing a strategic strategy to attain it.

Continue innovating

When you're working toward your goal of having a profession where you do what you love, you will meet setbacks and failure — that's unavoidable. The goal is to transform such losses into achievements by concentrating on continual and strategic innovation. How can you refine your approach? How can you adjust what you're doing to more promptly reach your goal?

If you're not sure what method to adopt, try utilizing all three: committing to innovation in your professional life with the support of a coach or mentor. Research suggests that this combination of dedication and mentoring is one of the most successful strategies to develop a career in which you do what you love. Thirty years of study on the issue analyzed 43 studies comparing career outcomes of those who either engaged mentors or didn't in their quest for career innovation. Those who engaged mentors obtained greater salaries, and more promotions felt more content with (and committed to) their employment,t and were more likely to experience future professional progress. Another poll of 170 professionals indicated that those who engaged mentors were substantially more likely to respect their place of work and its leadership. Engaging a mentor also improved employee retention rates and employees' feeling of inclusion in the workplace, all of which come into play in terms of career satisfaction.

2. Develop positive habits

It may take a long for you to do what you love at work and earn a livelihood doing it, so you need to make sure you're creating sustainable habits throughout the process. This requires high-level habits, like being a strong networker and frequently attending seminars to develop your abilities, and personal ones, like knowing you're getting enough time off to do what you enjoy outside of work, like listening to engaging podcasts and spending with your children. When performed frequently throughout time, these behaviors will sustain you even when circumstances go difficult. As your professional adventure unfolds, you may always fall back on these gained and nurtured talents.

Developing good habits can also help you develop a healthy work-life balance, which will in turn boost your emotions of happiness once you are in a profession in which you enjoy what you do.
How does balancing your personal and professional life boost your career? Research reveals that it is work-life balance, not money, autonomy, or even recognition, that ultimately determines job success. Specifically, a poll of 4,100 corporate leaders from

medium-to-large organizations in 33 countries indicated that, when workers can balance their professional and personal life, they engage considerably more easily with the tasks at hand (and the team with whom they cooperate) than overworked employees. This sense of work-life balance leads not just to fewer exits from a specific firm but also to workers feeling like they "have it all" in terms of holistic life satisfaction. Take their lead and attempt to integrate your job life with your personal life.

3. Increyour your passion for business by falling in love with your client

No matter how much love for the company you build, there will still be duties you don't like and days when you doubt your business concept. What keeps you going through moments like this and helps you continue to enjoy what you do? Jay says that having a job where you do what you love is a question of falling in love with your customers.

When you take the emphasis off your goods and services and place it on how your company impacts the lives of individuals you serve, you may enjoy what you do even during the most tedious chores.

Jay advises you need to abandon the urge to make your firm the "biggest" or "most popular" and instead be enthusiastic about the influence you have on your clients' lives. Make each encounter you have with consumers an opportunity to learn more about their beliefs, goals, and ambitions and become their trusted counsel for how to acquire what they want. When you recognize your customer's life is your business life, you understand that falling in love with them sparks your enthusiasm for the business.

Being able to do what you love for a job is doable, but it takes time. Decide now to start working toward your objectives, and recognize that there are numerous milestones along the path between where you started and where you want to be. Most essential, create habits that fill your life with pleasure as you journey along the road to success.

4. Give yourself credit for wanting to do what love love

Making change requires guts, and that's precisely what you're doing when you take measures to pursue what you love. Instead of settling for the status quo, you've chosen the high road to create a life that inspires you.

5. Appreciate your mistakes

Learning how to do what you love is a process. Resist the temptation to look at your present profession as a failure or error. Instead, look at it as a source of knowledge - on what you don't want to be doing for a livelihood, the abilities you gained in the course of your employment, and the network you've formed. When you're able to learn from your errors without beating yourself up over them (or throwing up the towel) (or throwing in the towel), every step you take is a step toward a life where you love what you do.

You deserve to have a fulfilling career that allows you to do what you love for a living. Unearth your inner potential and deepest talents with our Business Identity quiz. Discover and utilize your gift to find your ultimate calling in life.

Chapter 3

Building your career

Having a good job will provide you with a lot of perks and actual earning prospects. As we live in a society driven by social status and money, working your way up to the top will enhance your quality of life. There are numerous different reasons why a person may seek success.

I suppose one of the reasons is that maybe being successful in your work life helps you feel better among other people. It provides you with a sense of security and success. Many individuals who went from zero to a great job have remarked that their lives were enhanced in practically all areas.

There are some behaviors and practices that successful individuals from all over the globe do. The ideal method of approaching success is by following and finding out what the tactics that pros employ, then replicating them according to your requirements.

The following seven working tactics will provide you with adequate boosts to enhance your profession.

1. Highlight Your Goals

Before ever contemplating taking a professional track, you must learn to know yourself. A great majority of individuals travel through life by following a well-established pattern. The terrible aspect is, that they don't even enjoy what they do or they simply don't recognize how many other things they could do.

To prevent this dreadful occurrence, you need to understand what are your largest sensible desires. Then, start digging deeper and perform an in-depth reflection in which you should think about the relationship between your inner wants and your reasonable aims.

They have to match. Otherwise, you would not be fully pleased with your work life. Identifying your objectives takes some time and work, but it is a genuinely crucial aspect of any successful person's path.

2. Develop a Professional Resume

Your CV is your method of expressing "I'm excellent at this, good at that, and I can assist by doing this and that". Well, that is why you should build a professional, clean CV.

By taking care of this issue, you are making sure that you'll never be caught off guard. Opportunities are available, and you should always be ready with a solid CV. I feel that having specialists work with your CV is a fruitful decision.

There are several excellent services like Careers Booster or Visual CV that may take care of your difficulty. They may enable you to develop a classic or attractive graphic CV.

3. Able to Identify your strengths

Awareness is a vital aspect of personal progress. By being conscious of your inner thoughts, your strengths, your desires, and your shortcomings, you can adjust your life to whatever situations you're being put through. You'll also obtain several advantages as you may utilize your knowledge and expertise for the greatest goals.

It's best if you select your long-term vocation according to what you know about yourself. Are you a patient person? Would you be able to sit for eight to twelve hours at an office working on a computer? Or you'd rather be a football coach because you're sincerely enthusiastic about football and you feel you might be an effective trainer?

No of your skills and shortcomings, you should select a job path that favors your attributes and talents.

4. Assume Full Responsibility for Your Life

One distinction between average and successful professionals: is accountability. Even while you know the principle, you may not implement it every day. Whenever anything horrible occurs, you need to assume it.

Even if you haven't done anything illegal, being there and e, the past decisions you've made (like trusting someone), are still all elements that have been impacted by your thoughts and actions.

Start embracing responsibility for all of your activities and never blame anybody for your faults. That's the worst thing someone can do. Do not take anything personally, and remain cool.

5. Always Raise Your Standards

Here's another key aspect that divides the successful from the non-successful. Your standards impact the way you think, believe, and conduct. If your expectations are high, you'll never be happy with less than you can do. People with high standards are most of the time more successful than the norm.

Every two or three months take a minute to reflect on your standards and values. Try to enhance them little by bit up until you discover that you've become the best version of yourself.

6. Brand Yourself

Branding is crucial today. Big firms are spending hundreds of millions to position themselves as the "big dogs" in the marketplace. It is an ancient business approach employed by practically every professional corporation. Your branding is your picture in the marketplace.

Professional staff should brand their identities and services and continually enhance them. You may achieve it by launching a blog, developing a professional social media presence, or simply delivering excellent services.

7. Network — A LOT

Networking is all about possibilities and relationships. When you meet new individuals, you have an opportunity to leverage their expertise to your benefit. Of course, you must also offer back something: your skills, your expertise, your money. Successful individuals constantly network and develop those life-lasting beneficial partnerships.

Start by establishing social media accounts on LinkedIn, Twitter, and Facebook. These three specialized networks are the finest alternatives when it comes to this sort of activity. You'll discover tons of possibilities and career alternatives along the road.

LinkedIn, for example, is loaded with business people that are branding their company and also networking at the same time. Twitter is also extensively utilized in these topics, and Facebook... Facebook is useful for everything, including networking.

Chapter 4

Networking

Networking helps a professional stay up with current developments in the sector and creates contacts that may increase future business or job possibilities.

What is Networking?

Networking is the exchanging of information or services between individuals, corporations, or organizations. It is also a tool for people to improve their ties with their profession or company. As a consequence, connections or a network may be created and valuable for people in their professional or personal life. Networking helps develop meaningful connections that are advantageous to all involved parties in the flow of information and services. Gaining new key business connections may be acquired via networking meetings, social media, personal networking, and business networking.

In the second part of the twentieth century, networking was advocated to enable business people to grow their social capital. In the US, workplace equality advocates advocated business networking by members of underrepresented groups (e.g., women, African-Americans, etc.) to identify and overcome the hurdles limiting them from professional achievement. Mainstream business literature eventually accepted the phrases and ideas and touted them as roads to success for all career climbers.

Types of networking

1. Casual contact networks

These are generic business organizations that accept numerous persons from many overlapping professions.
These clubs normally meet monthly and frequently conduct mixers where everyone mingles casually.
They may also host meetings where guest speakers lecture on significant business themes or address problems impacting legislation, a community affair,s or local business activities.

The clearest examples of these associations are the hundreds of chambers of commerce operating throughout North America and elsewhere in the globe.
They provide participants with a chance to develop crucial relationships with many other entrepreneurs in the neighborhood. By attending chamber events, you may create beginning relationships that will be beneficial in other elements of growing your referral company.

But, since casual-contact groups aren't intended particularly to help you acquire recommendations, you have to take an effort to make them work. For example, you may volunteer to be a chamber ambassador, a position that involves minimal time commitment but gives significant exposure. Sitting in committees lets you get to know people better. Most of all, you need to attend events consistently so you can take advantage of every chance to build the connections you make.

2. Strong contact networks

Organizations whose mission is main to assist members to exchange business recommendations are known as strong contact referral organizations.
Some of these organizations meet regularly, generally over lunch or breakfast. Most of them restrict membership to one person per profession or specialization.

Strong contact networks give highly concentrated options for you and your partners to begin creating your referral marketing efforts. You won't meet hundreds of businesses in this sort of gathering, but all the participants will be carrying your business cards around with them wherever they go.

The overall outcome is like having up to 50 salesmen working for you! With a program like this, you'll be developing strong long-term partnerships that will be priceless.

If you're contemplating a strong-contact group, you'll want to keep a few things in mind:

You need to establish a schedule that enables you to attend all or virtually all of the meetings.

Regular attendance is crucial to building a connection with the other members of the group and getting to know their companies.

You need to feel comfortable attending a networking event and being on the lookout for prospects who can aid other members of your organization. A solid strong-contact networking organization often records the quantity of business that's transacted. If you're not "pulling your weight," you'll be asked to leave or recommendations will stop coming your way.

3. Community service clubs

Unlike more business-oriented clubs, service groups aren't put up solely for referral networking; their activities are centered on service to the community. However, while donating time and effort to civic concerns, you create permanent contacts that widen and strengthen your personal and commercial networks. If you go in not to gain but to contribute, the social capital you build will ultimately repay you in other ways and from other angles — business among them.

Chapter 5

Teamwork makes the dream work

Teamwork makes the dream work implies when a group of folks gather together to create a team and have their hearts and minds focused on a desired goal or purpose, accomplishing that objective will be feasible when everyone on the team works together.

Why Teamwork Makes The Dream Work?

So why is teamwork important? Teamwork makes the dream a reality because groups are more likely to succeed than individuals. Team building exercises offer various advantages, including strengthening communication and problem-solving abilities so that operations within the work environment operate more smoothly.

Motivation

Motivation to be productive and generate excellent service is vitally crucial to the success of your organization. Team building exercises provide workers with a fresh feeling of vitality. It helps them feel as if they are vital to the team and the organization, which in turn pushes them to achieve.

Continuous learning also encourages individuals. Even if they don't recognize it, practically everyone has a persistent need for knowledge. Working on knowledge-based tasks in team-building exercises will make people feel that they are worth the investment and they will be inspired to engage since they instantly receive something out of it.

Breaking Barriers

There are all various forms of obstacles in the job. There are physical barriers like walls and cubicles that keep individuals isolated throughout their everyday activities. But there are also a lot of emotional and symbolic hurdles.

Barriers such as various employment levels and departments, as well as barriers between different sorts of people, genders, ethnicities, and socioeconomic positions, may all come between individuals and impede teams from operating effectively.

Team building activities can help break through such boundaries. When you are investing in team development, everyone is on a level playing field. Everyone participates equally, and workers who would usually keep to themselves will learn that they work effectively with the other individuals in their department or firm.

Also, managers who equally engage in team-building activities are better integrated into their teams. When managers are regarded as normal individuals a various work levels, they become more personal and likable. This may make following the management more natural, pleasant, and productive for workers inside the teams.

Enjoyment

Team building should always be pleasurable. If your workers feel coerced into participating and feel uneasy throughout the process, you're going to lose out on a lot of the advantages that it may provide. Also, you want staff to like their employment. When you engage in team building, you bring people closer together, which may make their employment and workplace a lot more fun place to be. This will enhance productivity as well.

Skill Improvement

Team building activities are also a wonderful method to brush up on skills that your staff may be missing or need a refresher. If you have one or a few workers who are exceptional with the abilities you need your team to thrive in, you can engage them to lead the rest of the team in activities that brush up those talents for everyone.

Not only can this assist boost performance and productivity, but it will also enable your staff to know who they can go to for support. When workers assist one another in this manner, it helps remove some of the strain off of management, which may free up managers to also be more productive and get more completed in a day.

Communication

To gather collaboration to make the dream work, communication is important. You'll want to incorporate lots of team-building activities that concentrate on how to transmit messages to each other successfully. Everyone has a particular communication style and unique linguistic style that they employ while conversing informally. It is crucial to include communication in team development so that workers may understand how each other communicates and put that information to use during work hours.

But communication isn't only about what is said; it's also about how it is conveyed. A great team has an energy, a buzz that you can almost feel palpable. One researcher wanted to find out what causes that buzz. The research findings demonstrated that how teams communicate-their tone of voice, and how much they speak and listen-plays a big impact on the performance of the team.

Problem Solving

One of the key takeaways from team building is problem-solving skills. Problem-solving is significantly simpler inside a team context than with people working alone. When team building exercises concentrate on having to work together to solve an issue, it helps workers learn how to depend on one another and work together to come up with answers.

Every company has its obstacles and thinking outside the box is a necessity for success. Team building activities that apply these ideas in a fun manner have workers working together to creatively solve issues quickly and efficiently.

Bonding

A more personal feel in the office may make workers feel more comfortable, less worried, happier, and ultimately more productive. The easiest method to acquire that personal feel in your firm is via low-key team development. You may do things like going to a baseball game or meeting up for a happy hour so that workers are not required to accomplish anything, but they have time to engage with one another and build those key interpersonal bonds.

www.ingramcontent.com/pod-product-compliance
Lightning Source LLC
LaVergne TN
LVHW020527160826
845677LV00015B/3937

* 9 7 9 8 8 4 8 6 9 8 3 1 2 *